Anonymous

Chisholm's Stranger's illustrated guide to the city of Montreal

Being a synopsis of its history, statistics, etc., and a thorough guide to its

drives, public buildings, public works, and resorts with a fine colored map

of the city

Anonymous

Chisholm's Stranger's illustrated guide to the city of Montreal
Being a synopsis of its history, statistics, etc., and a thorough guide to its drives,
public buildings, public works, and resorts with a fine colored map of the city

ISBN/EAN: 9783337775339

Printed in Europe, USA, Canada, Australia, Japan

Cover: Foto ©ninafisch / pixelio.de

More available books at **www.hansebooks.com**

Stranger's
ILLUSTRATED GUIDE

TO THE

CITY OF MONTREAL,

BEING A SYNOPSIS OF IT. HISTORY, STATISTICS, ETC., AND A
THOROUGH GUIDE TO ITS DRIVES, PUBLIC BUILDINGS,
PUBLIC WORKS, AND RESORTS.

ALSO GIVING THE

CARRIAGE TARIFF, DISTANCES, AND PARTICULARS

OF DIFFERENT OUTWARD

Railroad and Steamboat Routes ;

WITH A FINE

COLORED MAP OF THE CITY,

Showing the Distance from the Centre to the Different Points.

PRICE - - - 25 CENTS.

Montreal:
C. R. CHISHOLM & CO.
PUBLISHERS.
1870.

MECHANICS' INSTITUTE—See page 50.

CHISHOLM'S
Stranger's
ILLUSTRATED GUIDE

TO THE

CITY OF MONTREAL,

BEING A SYNOPSIS OF ITS HISTORY, STATISTICS, ETC., AND A
THOROUGH GUIDE TO ITS DRIVES, PUBLIC BUILDINGS,
PUBLIC WORKS, AND RESORTS.

ALSO GIVING THE

CARRIAGE TARIFF, DISTANCES, AND PARTICULARS

OF DIFFERENT OUTWARD

Railroad and Steamboat Routes;

WITH A FINE

COLORED MAP OF THE CITY,

Showing the Distance from the Centre to the Different Points.

PRICE - - - 25 CENTS.

Montreal:
C. R. CHISHOLM & CO.
PUBLISHERS.
1870.

CONTENTS.

———•❦•———

STREET GUIDE.

NOTICE TO READERS.

On entering any street, when you find out its name, look at the following STREET
INDEX, *and it will point out the page on which the description of that street
and its buildings is to be found:*

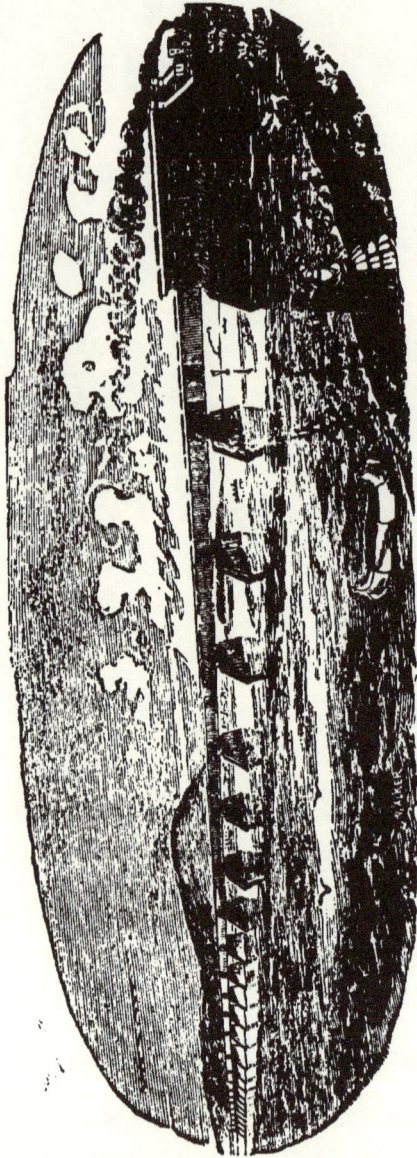

VICTORIA BRIDGE, MONTREAL.—THE LONGEST BRIDGE IN THE WORLD

See page 61.

MONTREAL:

A SKETCH OF ITS HISTORY, STATISTICS, ETC., ET

GOING back a period of 320 years, we seem to see JACQUES CARTIER, whose name is ever memorable in the history of Canada, on the 3rd of October, 1535, entering for the first time the little Indian village of "Hochelaga," the germ or nucleus of first, the town of Mount Royal, and so, of the city of Montreal;—eventful visit this, fraught with great results. We can sympathize with the emotions which would fill the mind of the explorer, as he gazed around on "the beautiful panorama of thirty leagues radius, that stretched out of the view from the eastern promontory of the mountain;" and yet we cannot suppress a feeling of pity, as we think of the fate of those simple yet valiant sons of the forest, who gathered round Cartier, as if before a superior being, and whose race has been so sternly driven back by the steady advance of civilization. But we may not pause upon this subject, and so we ask our visitors and citizens to recognise, if they can, the features of the following picture of ancient Montreal, in the substantial stone and brick of our modern architecture :—

"The way to the village was through large fields of Indian corn. "Its outline was circular; and it was encompassed by three separate "rows of palisades, or rather picket fences, one within the other, well "secured and put together. A single entrance was left in this rude "fortification, but guarded with pikes and stakes, and every precaution "taken against siege or attack. The cabins or lodges of the inhabi- "tants, about fifty in number, were constructed in the form of a tunnel, "each fifty feet in length by fifteen in breadth. They were formed of "wood covered with bark. Above the doors of the houses as well as "along the outer rows of the palisades, ran a gallery ascended by ladders, "where stones and other missiles were ranged in order for the defence "of the place. Each house contained several chambers, and the whole "were arranged so as to enclose an open court yard, where the fire was "made."

Again we pass on over 200 years, with all their whirl of exciting events; and in 1760, the date of British possession, we find Montreal a well peopled town, "of an oblong form, surrounded by a wall flanked "with eleven redoubts, which served instead of bastions. The ditch "was about eight feet deep and of a proportionable breadth, but dry; "it had also a fort, or citadel, the batteries of which commanded the "streets of the town from one end to the other."

Coming to more modern dates, we find that though the city was increasing in population, and augmenting its trade; yet a New York writer, some forty-five years ago, thus characterized Montreal:—"The "approach to Montreal conveyed no prepossessing idea of the enterprise "of its municipality; ships, brigs and steamboats lay on the margin of "the river at the foot of a hill. No long line of wharves built of the "substantial free stone, of which there is abundance in the neighbour-"hood, afforded security to vessels and owners; the commercial haven "looked as ragged and as muddy as the shores of New Nederland when "the Guedevrow first made her appearance off the Battery."

McGregor, too, in his British America, a work of not very ancient date, thus described Montreal:—"Betwixt the Royal Mountain and the "River, on a ridge of gentle elevation, stands the town. * * * * "There are no wharves at Montreal, and the ships and steamers lie "quietly in pretty deep water, close to the clayey and generally filthy "bank of the city."

Such then was our city in times bygone. In the days of our fathers, no stately steam-ships ferried us across the Atlantic, no floating palaces conveyed us safely, speedily, and securely up and down our noble St. Lawrence, and across, as the "Times" has fitly termed it, "that magnificent series of inland seas, the high road from Europe to the North American continent." Then, no great chain of railway linked town to town, and city to city, almost annihilating distance. Then, the journey to Detroit was a toilsome matter of several weeks; and that to Brockville, short even as is the distance, occupied, with heavy cumbrous *batteaux*, three weeks. Now how changed! The wand of some fairy king has surely been here. No! but industry, intelligence, labour, capital, all combined, and working for the advancement of this rising colony, have produced the marvellous changes which meet us on ever, hand.

This, the largest and most populous city in British North America, and the commercial capital of the Province, was founded in 1642, under the name of "Ville-Marie," near the site of the Indian village of "Hochelaga." The name was afterwards changed to "Mount Royal," from the mountain which overlooks the city. It is situated on an island bearing the same name, in the combined embrace of the Ottawa and St. Lawrence,—which latter river at this point is upwards of a mile and a half wide,—180 miles S. W. of Quebec, 420 miles N. of New York, and about 800 miles from the sea. It possesses, partly from its latitude, and partly from the great area of water with which it is surrounded, a mildness and softness of climate unknown to any other part of the Province of Quebec, is the largest island in Canada, being 32 miles long and 10½ miles wide, and is considered the garden of the Lower Provinces. Its area is 197 square miles. The soil is in most parts excellent, and produces nearly every kind of grain, fruit, and vegetable in perfection. The surface is level, with the exception of the mountain near the city; it is, however, diversified by several gentle ridges, having a tendency from N. E. to S. W., which are designated coteaux. The main branch of the Ottawa, which is the lumber highway to Quebec, passes North of the island, and enters the St. Lawrence about 18 miles below the city; about one-third of its waters are, however, discharged into Lake St. Louis, and joining but not mingling at Caughnawaga, the two distinct bodies pass over the Sault St. Louis and the Lachine Rapids—the dark waters of the Ottawa washing the quays of the city of Montreal, while the blue St. Lawrence laves the opposite shore. Nor do they merge their distinctive character until they are several miles below the city. The quays of Montreal are unsurpassed by those of any city in America; built of solid limestone, and uniting with the locks and cut stone wharves of the Lachine Canal, they present for several miles a display of masonry which has few parallels. Unlike the levees of the Ohio and Mississippi, no unsightly warehouses disfigure the river side. A broad terrace, faced with gray limestone, the parapet of which is surmounted by a substantial iron railing, divides the city from the river throughout its whole extent. In the summer months the scene on the harbour is full of life and interest. There are over one hundred and fifty-six miles of streets and lanes in the city.

Of these, a large number are watered daily during the summer months. In the rear of the city, running parallel to the river, at the distance of about a mile and a half from the water's edge, rises a long ridge of rocky and precipitous hill, some 700 feet in height, from which was derived the original name of the city, "Mount Royal." The summit of this mountain commands a view, extensive and diversified, of the city, with its towers, and spires, and public buildings, and a vast sweep of the surrounding country. In mid-river lies the umbrageous island of St. Helens—half park, half arsenal, glistening in the morning sun like an emerald set in gold. The St. Lawrence, a mile and a half wide at the narrowest point, extends east and west as far as the eye can reach, covered with ships fresh from the ocean, and by steamers numberless, leaving on the wind their marky trail. In mid-landscape, that architectural marvel, the Victoria Bridge, spans the river, in all its strength and beauty ; and the ear can detect the roar of each passing train which rushes through its iron ribs. Beyond, the rail-tracks wind through a champaign country, settled for two centuries, where farm dwellings and buildings line the roads like streets,—rich in population and rustic wealth ; while in the distance the twin mountains of Belœil and Montarville, sights even more picturesque than their names are musical, rise from the plain, like isles of beauty amid a sea of verdure. But the eye can hardly tear itself from the scene of cultivation close around. The slopes of the mountain, and the rich alluvial soil at its foot, are one entire garden. Villas and pleasure-grounds cover the hill-side. A beautiful reservoir, cleft out of the rock, glitters in the sunlight with all the formal beauty of a *paysage* by Watteau. The costumes and gay colours of the present day heighten the allusion, and impart health and freshness to the city spread beneath. In the distant valleys, the agricultural skill of the English farmer combines with old French minuteness and precision to create a scene

> " Ever changing, ever new :
> When will the landscape tire the view ?
> The fountain's fall ; the river's flow ;
> The woody valley, warm and low ;
> The windy summit, wild and high—
> Roughly reaching to the sky ;
> The pleasant seat ; the ruined tower ;
> The naked rock ; the shady bower ;
> The town—the village—dome—and far
> Each gives to each a double charm—
> Like pearls upon an Ethiop's arm."

But the spectator from the hill-top, or the frequenter of St. James Street, or of the Rue Notre Dame, must not suppose that in 1812, the year of the war with the United States, things were as they now are. Not for twenty-five years after, did a civic government provide for the wants of advancing civilization : not for twenty-five years did gas-lights or pavements, or hydrants exist. The long line of banks and stately edifices which now adorn St. James Street, rise from an abandoned graveyard, which in 1812 was bounded by the crumbling city defences. Fortification Lane was the foot of the town wall ; Craig Street was the town ditch ; beyond, on the upland, were country houses and orchards. In the same year, Notre Dame Street, now flashing with plate glass and the piled stores of jewellery and brocade, was a narrow street, of low, cosy Canadian houses, one storey and a half high—the *sancta* of much genial grace and of unbounded hospitality. The nocturnal reveller— and there was a good deal of revelry in those days—who slipped off the disjointed stones, mis-called *trottoirs*, plunged mid-leg in the mud, in the palpable darkness, without hope of refuge in a street railway-car, or of help from a sleepy policeman. The old Catholic parish church, which in early days gave a Catholic welcome to the churchless Protestant congregation, stood lengthwise in front of the site of the present noble church of Notre Dame—grand in design, though somewhat marred by a too great severity of style. Those splendid wharves faced with miles of cut stone, unequalled in America, and rivalled only in Europe by the docks of Liverpool, or the quays of St. Petersburg, have replaced a nauseous bank, heaped with filth and garbage, a muddy islet, the recep tacle of driftwood and drowned animals, and a turbid stream, from whence the strongest swimmer never rose. Montreal of the present day, with its palatial residences,—its places of public resort,—markets, numerous, convenient, and ornamental,—with its cathedrals, churches, colleges, convents,—with its multiplied institutions and social improvements,—with a population of over 130,000 souls, is as superior to the Montreal of 1840 as the Montreal of 1840 was in advance of the Montreal of 1812, yet at that time it was the commercial heart of Canada ; the fountain of supply ; the focus of mercantile energy and wealth ; and was regarded as the grand end and aim—the promised prize of American conquest. It was favourably situated for intercourse with the Upper Province, New York and Boston, being at the head of the ordinary navigation of the Atlantic, and at the foot of the grand chain of canals, which connect the great lakes Ontario, Erie, Huron and Superior with the river and the ocean. It is also connected by railroad and steamboat with all parts of Canada and the United States.

Montreal is the port at which arrives the great bulk of the importations from Great Britain and other places abroad, which are there either re-sold or transhipped to all parts of the Provinces of Ontario and Quebec and the United States.

A large wholesale and manufacturing trade is carried on in Montreal in all descriptions of goods; the manufacture of boots and shoes particularly has risen to a great prominence, and many persons engaged in the business have rapidly acquired wealth. The wholesale trade is in the hands of some ten or a dozen houses. The amount of capital invested in all the works is over $750,000, and the number of boots and shoes of all kinds manufactured, average upwards of 9,000,000 from each factory. This branch of trade gives constant employment to over 1,500 persons, many of whom, of course, are women and children.

The city and suburbs are lighted with gas, and many of the principal streets paved with stone. From whichever side approached, Montreal and its vicinity—the wood-clad " Mount Royal " forming a magnificent background, with its numerous beautiful villas, orchards, and delightful drives, its grand spires and lofty towers—present to the view of the beholder a vast, picturesque, and grand panorama.

Montreal also abounds in societies and institutions, national, benevolent, literary, and scientific, the most important of which will be noticed further on in their proper places.

The population of Montreal is a very trustworthy remembrancer of its varied history, being composed of the descendants of the ancient lords of the soil and their British successors, in proportions which are every year becoming more nearly equal.

The press of Montreal is also an index to its twofold inhabitants. There are in the two languages about 30 publications of various kinds.

ST. ANDREW'S CHURCH—See page 17.

PUBLIC BUILDINGS, SQUARES, &c.

ALEXANDER STREET (see St. Alexander)

BEAVER HALL HILL.

ZION CHURCH (*Congregational*). At the corner of Latour street. This church, which was not long since almost totally destroyed by fire, has been re-erected. It is a neat building in the Doric style of architecture ; is estimated to seat 1,250 persons comfortably. It has lately been much enlarged by an addition in rear, consisting of Vestry and Committee rooms, and accommodation for the "Congregational College," which has been removed from Kingston, Ont. Rev. Henry Wilkes, D.D., pastor.

BAPTIST CHURCH (FIRST). On the corner of Lagauchetiere street. A new and rather pleasing looking building, of a Gothic style; will accommodate about 750 persons. Rev. John Alexander, minister.

ST. ANDREW's CHURCH (C. of S.). This church, which was nearly demolished by fire in the Fall of 1869, but has since been rebuilt, is a beautiful specimen of the Gothic style of architecture; is an ornament to the city, and is worthy to be called an ecclesiastical structure. The tower and spire are good, the mouldings are bold and well cut, and the windows in keeping. The interior is well arranged and handsomely fitted up, and will accommodate upwards of 1,000 persons. The church is enclosed on three sides with a railing of cast and wrought iron, on a cut-stone plinth. The railing is divided into compartments by massive stone pillars, and, together with the plinth, is of a design corresponding in style with the church; which, by-the-by, is also used by the Scotch soldiers of the Garrison.

CHURCH OF THE MESSIAH (*Unitarian*). Opposite the above is a plain and substantial edifice, in the Byzantine style of architecture, which also suffered by fire last year (1869). The tower is about seventeen feet square, and about 120 feet high. Over the west end entrance is a large rose window, and in the chancel another, both filled with highly decorative stained glass. The church, which is under the ministry of the Rev. John Cordner, affords accommodation for over 750 persons.

B

BELMONT STREET.

NORMAL AND MODEL SCHOOLS. The building in which the above-named schools are held is a rather handsome pile in the Tudor style of architecture. This institution is intended to give a thorough training to teachers, which end is satisfactorily attained by instruction and training in the Normal, and by practice in the Model Schools. Professor W. H. Hicks is principal of this institution.

BERTHELET STREET

THE LADIES' BENEVOLENT INSTITUTION, for the relief of widows and half-orphans, is a large unpretending three-storey building. This Society, as its name infers, is managed solely by a committee of Ladies, and is one of the most useful in Canada.

BLEURY STREET.

ST. MARY'S COLLEGE (*Jesuit*). At the corner of Dorchester street is a large and handsome stone building, with an extensive play-ground for the use of the scholars, in front. Rev. Father Vignon, S. J., Director.

JESUITS' CHURCH. This fine building is 230 feet long and 102 feet wide, with a transept 152 feet long. The roof is supported by double rows of columns, terminating with composite capitals. There are no galleries, with the exception of an organ gallery, which, at each side of the organ, will accommodate the students and pupils of the College. The height of the middle nave is 75 feet, and the width between the rows of columns is 40 feet. The height of the side naves is 34 feet. The rear wall of the chancel is octagonal, as are also the terminal walls of the transept. The chancel and transept are lighted by immense ornamental windows. The ceiling is beautifully frescoed and the walls adorned with magnificent paintings of scenes in evangelical and ecclesiastical history. There is accommodation for over 4,500 persons. The basement, unlike the generality of Roman Catholic churches, consists of a large amphitheatre and forum, capable of seating 4,000 persons. The height is twenty feet above the forum, and 11 feet in front. The entrance to the church is by two large, handsome towers, which open on a vestibule 17 feet deep, and extending across the entire front of the church. These towers are about 200 feet high, and 30 feet square, and present a corner instead of a face to the street.

BONSECOURS STREET.

SOLDIERS' INSTITUTE, is a stone building on the corner of Champ de Mars street, and is an institution worthy of support, the intention being to draw the soldier from the tavern, and lower places of resort.

It contains Reading Room, Library, and Billiard Room, besides conveniences for many other amusements.

CHENNEVILLE STREET.

JEWISH SYNAGOGUE, is a neat cut stone building, the interior of which is beautifully fitted up in the Egyptian style. Rev. A. De Sola, Rabbi.

COLLEGE STREET.

ASHES INSPECTION STORE, is a large brick building, extending nearly as far back as William street; all the inspection of Pots and Pearls for the city trade, which is pretty extensive, is done here by Messrs. Dyde & Major.

ROMAN CATHOLIC COLLEGE, a plain, substantial pile of buildings, well suited to the purpose originally intended. Of late, however, it has been used as a barracks. The 60th Rifles occupied it during their service in Canada.

COMMISSIONERS STREET.

ST. ANN's MARKET, is a neat brick building, consisting of butchers', traders', and green-grocers' stalls, with a large hall above the butchers' market, used by Mr. Wm. Evans, as the Lower Canada Agricultural Hall ; was built at a cost of about 12,000, on the site of the old Government House

COMMON STREET.

TIME BALL. Coming along the river side the stranger is attracted to a rather curious looking apparatus on the roof of Messrs. Boyer & Hudon's store. This turns out to be a time regulator for the shipping public, which is governed from the McGill Observatory by electricity, and descends punctually every day at noon.

CUSTOM HOUSE SQUARE, in the centre of which stands the old " Custom House." In front of the building is a small enclosure filled with flowers and shrubs, and having a fountain in its midst. On the left is the Montreal House. In the adjoining block are the offices of the Trinity Board and the Harbour Commissioners ; on the opposite side are some fine warehouses.

ROYAL INSURANCE BUILDING, at the junction of this with Commissioners street, the palatial magnificence of which cannot fail to attract the beholder, is a fine building, a credit to the city, being erected in a most sumptuous style. The elevations are of a more or less elaborate design. The handsomest portion of the building is the tower, which contains a fine four-faced clock, and is surmounted by a cupola, covered with zinc, in fish-scale pattern. The court, the walls of which are lined with white

Dutch tiles, a novel feature in this country, presents a very light, clear and handsome appearance, while the ornamental iron railing and columns surrounding the galleries, bronzed and painted a rich cobalt colour, give it altogether a cool and chaste character. The fitting of the offices of the " Royal Insurance Company," of carved oak throughout, and in keeping with the architecture of the building, are, without exception, the most handsome in the city. The building is divided by four fire-proof brick partitions.

MONTREAL OCEAN S. S. COMPANY'S OFFICE, belonging to the Messrs. H. & A. Allan, situated at the junction of this and Youville streets, is a substantial and ornamental cut stone building. At the wharf below is generally to be seen one or more of the Company's steamers loading or unloading their cargoes alongside the large freight sheds, erected for their accommodation.

COTTE STREET.

THEATRE ROYAL is outwardly a very plain building. The interior is fitted up to seat about 1,750 persons.

SCHOOL OF THE CHRISTIAN BROTHERS (*Friars*) is a large cut-stone building, attended principally by French Canadian children, who pay but a nominal amount for tuition. The C. B. deserve great credit for their efforts to educate the young of their own religion, by opening schools in all parts of the city.

PRESBYTERIAN CHURCH OF CANADA (*Free*), is a neat and comfortably fitted up cut-stone edifice. A high tin-covered spire, and a flight of stone steps with iron railing in front, add greatly to its appearance. Will accommodate about 1000 persons. Rev. Dr. Burns, pastor.

CRAIG STREET.

This street was formerly the course of a rivulet or town ditch, which has been converted into a tunnel, forming a large and useful main sewer, to carry off the waste water. It now forms one of the widest streets and greatest thoroughfares of the city.

CATTLE MARKET, is a large and well adapted brick building, containing offices, weigh-house, and clerk's residence.

FRENCH PROTESTANT CHURCH, on the corner of Elizabeth street, is in size 60 x 40, of rough stone, with cut-stone dressings, in the early English style of architecture, with pointed windows, and an octagonal canopied spire. There is a basement under the entire length of the edifice, 10 feet high, well lighted and ventilated. The buildings in connection with and adjoining the church are a Bible Depository on the same street, and the pastor's residence on St. Elizabeth street, both

having cut-stone fronts and pointed windows. Rev. R. P. Duclos, pastor.

THE MILITARY SCHOOL, situated on this street, just opposite the Champ de Mars, is a spacious structure, well adapted to the purpose for which it is designed. There are apartments for arms, ammunition, and other military equipments. Cost, $100,000.

CENTRAL HOSE STATION, a fine three-storey stone and brick building, at the corner of Chenneville street, was erected for the Corporation by Mr. M. H. Perrault, in 1863. It has accommodation in the third storey for the Chief Engineer.

THE ROOMS OF THE YOUNG MEN'S CHRISTIAN ASSOCIATION,— with their excellent Library, &c., are at the corner of Craig and Alexander streets.

ST. PATRICK'S HALL, situated at the corner of Craig street and Victoria square, is a fine monument of the energy, taste, and patriotism of the Irishmen of Montreal. The building has a frontage of 140 feet on Victoria square, and 100 on Craig street and Fortification lane. The height from the street level to the cornice is 72 feet. In the early part of March, 1869, a portion of the roof unfortunately gave way and fell in. A thorough restoration has, however, been effected, and some improvements made in the interior arrangements.

DALHOUSIE STREET.

ST. STEPHEN'S CHURCH (C. of E.), in the style of the 13th century, and similar in appearance to St. George's, yet with somewhat less pretensions. The interior is arranged in a neat, comfortable manner. The church is in size about 100 by 55 feet, and will seat over 1200 persons. A number of the sittings are free. Rev. Mr. Curran, minister.

DORCHESTER STREET.

ST. LUKE'S CHURCH (C. of E.) In the east of this street is a neat stone edifice, well finished within and without. This church was erected immediately after the great fire of 1852. The building will seat about 800 persons, and is under the pastoral care of the Rev. James Thorncloe.

MONTREAL GENERAL HOSPITAL, better known as the "English Hospital," on the corner of St. Dominique street, is an elegant and commodious cut stone building. The management of the institution is admirable, and has been the means of conferring an immense amount of good on all classes. It is divided into wards, each for a specified ailment, and is under the direction of the best and most learned physicans in the city.

FRENCH MISSION CHURCH (*Protestant*), erected, as its name indicates, by the French Protestant Mission, is situated in this street, near the corner of St. Urbain, is built of brick with stone dressing and slate roof and is in the Gothic style of architecture. The church is 53 feet long by 30 wide. The pews are open, and afford accommodation for nearly 300. There is a commodious, well-lighted basement, adapted for either school or lecture room.

ST. JOHN THE EVANGELIST (C. of E.), at the corner of St. Urbain, a small brick building, with something of the Gothic style about it; is very neatly fitted up in the interior; a very handsome stained glass win-dow is the principal attraction. Rev. Edmund Wood, M. A., curate..

PROTESTANT HOUSE OF INDUSTRY AND REFUGE. This institution consists of two large, substantial looking brick buildings, near Bleury street. The building in front is 3 stories high, and measures 60 by 50 feet, forming that portion of the institution where the various offices, board room, superintendent's dwelling, &c., are situated. On the ground floor are two shops, a spacious entrance hall and staircase, giving access to the above-named rooms, which are on the second storey; above them in the third storey are dormitories for the more respectable portion of the community who may require temporary shelter, and who would not like to be placed in the "House of Refuge" proper, which latter is in the rear building, 60 feet by 40, connected with the front one by a covered corridor, and consists of, on the ground floor, a spacious kitchen,. with large cooking kitchen attached,—superintendent's office, separate reception rooms, and staircases for the male and female applicants,. closets, &c. On the second storey are the women's dormitories, with water closets, &c., attached; while the third storey contains similar accommodation for men. Laundry, drying-room; bath rooms for males and females; fuel cellars, &c., are all provided in the basement. The whole building is thoroughly heated by steam. The rooms are large, lofty, and well ventilated, and great care appears to have been taken to obtain that great desideratum in an institution of this kind, viz., to keep the two sexes totally separated, and at the same time to be so near the superintendent's apartments, as to be at all times under his imme-diate supervision.

HIGH SCHOOL, a fine brick building in the Grecian style; is under the Protestant Board of School Commissioners, and is noted throughout the Province as a first-class educational institution. Rector, Prof. H. A. Howe, LL.D.

ST. JAMES' CLUB HOUSE, on the corner of University Street, one of the finest buildings in British North America. The exterior is in keep-ing with the purpose for which it is intended, the principal façades being on Dorchester and University streets. The base, to a height of seven feet above the foot walk, is executed in Montreal limestone, rough-faced ashlar, with dressed mouldings and angles. The super-structure is in red brick, with Ohio stone cornices, window dressings, &c. ; the entrance, bay windows, and balconies, being built entirely of the latter material. The whole building is surmounted by a massive medallion cornice, from which rises the curved Mansard roof, covered with metal. An ornamental cast iron cresting railing surrounds the flat portions of the roof, from which place extensive views of the mountain and city can be obtained. The building, which is fitted up with every modern comfort and convenience, is heated throughout with steam.

St. Paul's Church (C. of S.) For size, beauty, and convenience, this is one of the most important of our city churches. It is cruciform in plan, with tower, stained windows, and the usual accessories of Gothic architecture. The capacity of the building is that of 1000 sittings on the ground floor —there being no galleries, except one for the organ and choir. Under this gallery, and on the same level with the church floor, are the minister's and elders' vestries, fitted up with every requisite for comfort and convenience. The transepts and nave are divided on either side of the church by an arcade of three arches, resting on octagonal pillars of Ohio stone, out of the capitals of which are worked the corbels for the support of the roof principals. There is a basement under the whole area of the church, divided into lecture rooms and school rooms, with the necessary adjuncts to each. The walls to the level of the base are constructed of Montreal limestone ; the super-structure is faced with similar material, having the natural surface of the stone exposed to view; the weatherings, groins, pinnacles, and all the ornamental parts of the work, are of Ohio sandstone. The roof is covered with slate from the Melbourne quarries. The internal dimensions of the nave are 102 by 69 feet : the transepts are about 46 feet wide, with a projection from the nave of nearly 17 feet. From the floor to the apex of the roof the height is 58 feet. Architects, Messrs. Lawford, Nelson & Hopkins. Pastor, Rev. Dr. Jenkins.

Knox Church (*Canada Presbyterian*). This building, which is situated at the corner of this and Mansfield Street, is chiefly frequented by the congregation lately worshipping in the old church in St. Gabriel street. It is in the early Gothic decorated style of architecture, the ashlar work of the walls, buttresses, &c., being built with small even courses of stone, having their natural face exposed ; the dressing of the windows and doors, the moulded work, &c., being chiselled. It is 110 feet in length by 60 in breadth, and consists internally of a nave and two side aisles, in the latter of which are galleries. The nave, arches, and roof are supported by light iron columns, which also support the galleries. The ceiling is plastered, and divided into panels by the roof timbers. There is an octagonal recess for the pulpit, over which there is a ground ceiling. The windows are filled with glass of a diaper pattern, with a stained margin around the different compartments; over the east gallery there is a large window filled with rich tracery. Great attention has been given to the heating and ventilating, which are carried out under the most approved system. The pews are arranged on a circular plan, and are calculated to accommodate nearly 800 persons. There are three entrances to the church, the principal one on this street being through a handsome open porch. There is a lofty and spacious basement, in which are a vestry, library, class-rooms, &c., &c. Pastor, Rev. Dr. Irvine.

WESLEYAN CHURCH is a fine building of the English Gothic style of architecture of the 13th century. The walls are stone throughout, the plain surface being natural faced work in small regular curves, and the angles and wreathings of buttresses, and the windows and door jams are of cut stone. The height of tower and spire is 170 feet. The basement is lofty and wholly above ground, and is divided into class and lecture rooms, lobbies, &c. The building is 61 feet by 93 feet clear, inside, and will accommodate about 800 persons. There are no galleries.

THE NEW CHURCH OF ST. GEORGE (C. of E.), situated on the corner of St. Janvier and St. Francis de Salles streets, near Dorchester, is a Montreal stone building, with the angles and moulded work in Ohio sandstone. The building has a large nave, 104 feet by 60 feet wide, under a single roof, with transepts on each side 45 feet by 24 feet deep, terminated with octagonal ends, as are the chancel and choir, which together are 40 feet deep by 27 feet wide. There is a large open porch forming entrance, with square tower on angle of building, which is intended to be finished with a spire, the total height of which from ground will be 240 feet. The building is in the decorated Gothic style, with traceried windows filled with stained glass. The ceiling will be lined with wood, which with the moulded principals supporting roof, are stained and varnished. The ornamental stained glass window at the end of the chancel, is to the memory of the late Metropolitan, Bishop Fulford ; and the one at right hand side of centre, to the memory of the late Hon. George Moffatt. The church will accommodate with gallery 1,300 persons; will cost, without the land, about $54,000. Architect, W. T. Thomas, Esq. The schools intended for this church are built on the same lot, fronting upon Stanley street, consist of day schools, with class rooms on ground floor, with large room on first floor 86 by 42. The buildings are of Montreal stone, roofs covered with slate, cost $12,000.

AMERICAN PRESBYTERIAN This building is an exact copy of Park Church in Brooklyn, N.Y., and has a massive appearance, no particular style being applied in the design. Its length over all is 144 feet, and the width 86 feet. The ceiling, a flat one, is 44 feet from the floor.

The front elevation on Dorchester street has two towers, one at each angle, the one next Drummond street finished with a spire rising to a height of 200 feet above the street, the other being finished square at about 80 feet high. The auditorum is 90 feet long by 76 feet wide, and, with the galleries, will seat 1,200 persons. There is no basement, the lecture and Sunday-school rooms being in the rear portion of the building, each being about 90 feet long by 30 feet wide. All the pews on the ground floor have a curved form, so that the minister can everywhere be seen without the listener sitting in an uneasy posture.

MONT STE. MARIE (*Nuns' School*), is a fine stone building in a commanding situation. From the top of a flight of stone steps leading to the main entrance, a fine view of the Victoria Bridge, with part of the city and surrounding country, may be obtained. The building was originally erected for a Baptist college, but has more recently been used as the St. Patrick's hospital, and is now used as a ladies' boarding school under the direction of the Congregational Nuns.

DRUMMOND STREET.

VICTORIA SKATING RINK, a neat brick building, with stone dressings, and roof of galvanized iron, having a frontage of 100 feet, and a depth of 250 feet, consisting of a large entrance hall, on each side of which there are dressing, hat, and cloak rooms. These rooms communicate with the rink, which covers an area of 16,160 superficial feet, and is surrounded by a promenade 10 feet wide, with a raised recess on one side for the band. The ice is spanned by a semi-circular arch-like roof, 50 feet high, which, springing from the ground, is so constructed as to give an apparent lightness of effect, combined with great strength, the surrounding walls being merely a casing as it were for the space. The building, which bears very much the appearance of an English railway station, is lighted at night by numerous gas jets, and is resorted to by the youth and beauty of our city, for whose use every convenience seems to have been taken into account.

FOUNDLING STREET.

GREY NUNNERY, or "General Hospital of Charitable Sisters," was founded in 1692, and after many vicissitudes became a flourishing institution. It is at present one of the most extensive charities in the city, being a foundling hospital, as well as a refuge for the infirm. The premises are surrounded by a wall, which extends as far back as Youville street, so called in memory of one of the foundresses of the hospital.

HANOVER STREET.

NEW JERUSALEM CHURCH, corner of this and Dorchester street, is a small brick building, the windows and doors of which are faced with cut stone. Rev. E. Gould, pastor.

LAGAUCHETIERE STREET.

WESLEYAN CHURCH. A large stone building on the corner of this and Durham street. This is the furthest east of the Wesleyan churches in the city, and is well attended.

COLLEGE OF PHYSICIANS AND SURGEONS (*French*), situated in this street, near St. Charles Borromee street, is a very unprepossessing building, surrounded by a common board fence. But albeit it has an unfavorable aspect, it has turned out some clever men from its halls.

THE CATHOLIC CONGREGATIONAL CHURCH, on the corner of Lagauchetiere and Chenneville streets, is a very plain looking edifice. The church was founded in 1833, as a United Presbyterian Church, but was rebuilt and enlarged in 1847. The former congregation of this church worship in the larger and much finer edifice in St. Catherine street, now called the Erskine Church.

ST. PATRICK'S CHURCH (*R. C.*), stands on an elevated site at the corner of St. Alexander street, and is one of the most striking objects visible on approaching the city. This large and commanding building is in the Gothic style of architecture. The length is 240 feet, by 90 feet in breadth ; the spire is 225 feet high. The interior is comfortably and handsomely fitted up, with room for over 5,000 worshippers. Taken altogether, this is a splendid model of ecclesiastical architecture.

THE R. C. BISHOP'S PALACE AND CHURCH, at the corner of Cemetery street, form the western limit of Lagauchetiere or Palace st.

M'CORD STREET.

ST. ANN'S CHAPEL, at the junction with Basin street, is a handsome stone building in the Gothic style of architecture, and will seat about 1,500 persons.

M'GILL STREET.

This will eventually be one of the finest thoroughfares in the city, on account of its great breadth and fine prospects at either extremity; having the Victoria Square and a distant glimpse of the mountain at one end, and a fine view of the river and the Victoria Bridge at the other. This street was formerly the boundary of the city proper; on the west and beyond lie Griffintown and the St. Antoine Suburb. There are a number of very fine stores in this street.

THE ALBION HOTEL is one of the ornaments of this street, Decker & Co., proprietors.

THE DOMINION AND ALBERT BUILDINGS cannot fail to attract the attention of the visitor to Montreal.

ST. PATRICK'S CHURCH—See page 28.

NOTRE DAME STREET.

DALHOUSIE SQUARE, at the head of this street, is occupied on the left as a cab stand, while on the right are a number of cut-stone dwelling houses, lately occupied as officers' quarters by the Royal Artillery and Engineers. The enclosure in front is very neatly fitted out with flowers, shrubs, &c., and a fountain in the centre.

The building known as the DONEGANA HOTEL, is large and handsome looking. It is now divided into offices for the various military departments.

GOVERNMENT GARDEN, is a handsomely decorated plot of ground belonging to Government, and leased by them to one of our principal seedsmen, Mr. George Shepherd, who seems to pay great attention to its cultivation.

The rooms of the INSTITUT CANADIEN will repay a visit. The most valuable books in the Library were the munificent gift of Prince Napoleon, who passed through Montreal some ten years ago.

JAQUES CARTIER NORMAL SCHOOL is a large building opposite the garden above mentioned. It is under the direction of R. C. Priests, and is well conducted. The offices of the Superintendent of Education for the Province of Quebec, were, until a few years ago, in the same building, which was once used as the Government House by the French governors.

JACQUES CARTIER SQUARE is a large open space extending from this street to the river. A magnificent view of the Victoria Bridge and St. Helen's Island is to be had from this square, which rises towards Notre Dame street with a considerable incline.

NELSON'S MONUMENT, situated at the head of the above square, is invariably visited by all strangers, and never fails to excite the deepest interest; on the pedestal *were* representations of three of the battles in which this gallant hero fought. We cannot refrain from saying that this column is a disgrace to the city. Through the culpable negligence of the corporation, the citizens, or both combined, the only public monument in the city, the only memorial to Great Britain's heroes which we can boast of, has been allowed to go to ruin; this which should be an honour to our city is a standing disgrace. And, as if to make this disgrace more palpable, Nelson's *back* is turned towards his natural element—the water. We regret to say that, in this matter, Englishmen have certainly *not* done their duty.

CHAMP DE MARS, or Military Parade Ground, is a fine gravelled space of 500 yards in length by 100 broad, and is bounded on one side by Craig street, and on the other by the Court House, the raised embankment in rear of which is well boarded, and a flight of steps leading to the parade ground and extending its entire length, furnishes a first rate *stand* for spectators.

COURT HOUSE. This is a large and stately pile of cut-stone buildings, in the Grecian Ionic style. The ground plan is 300 by 125 feet, and the height is 76 feet. The building contains large fire-proof vaults, fine Court-rooms for the Appeal, Circuit, Superior, Criminal, and Police Courts, and it also contains the offices of the Sheriff and Prothonotary, the Advocates' Room and Library, together with the different offices in connection with the several Courts. The whole building is heated with hot air, lighted with gas, and supplied with water and all other conveniences. At the end of the Court House, and in the small square leading to the Champ de Mars, is a small fountain, furnished with drinking cups.

BLACK NUNNERY, to reach which you must pass under an arch directly facing St. Lambert street. This is an educational establishment for French Canadian girls, in which all the branches of a general education, needle-work, music, embroidery, &c., are taught, all being under the direction of the Black Nuns. A large and handsome church has lately been erected on the grounds of the Nunnery.

PLACE D'ARMES, on French Square, is occupied in the centre by a pleasant enclosure, surrounded by a handsome iron railing, with gates at each corner, surmounted by stones bearing the city arms. The garden is laid out with shrubs and flower beds, having a rather pretty fountain in the midst, around which are placed seats, constituting a pleasant lounge.

ONTARIO BANK. This building, on the west side of Place d'Armes, is in the pure Italian style of Architecture, chaste and simple in its features, yet producing a handsome facade. It is four storeys high, and built of Montreal stone. The frontage of the building is fifty feet, and the depth seventy feet; height over sixty-two feet,—forming as a whole one of the finest buildings in the city.

CHURCH OF NOTRE DAME, generally, but improperly, called by British residents the " French Cathedral," is, in point of dimensions and area, the pride of Montreal. Its twin Gothic towers seen from afar off, bear no inconsiderable resemblance to that "Notre Dame " on the banks of the Seine. The corner stone of this edifice, which is built in the perpendicular Gothic style of the middle ages, was laid on the 3rd September, 1824, and was opened for public worship in July, 1829. It was originally intended to make it much larger than it is at present, in fact to extend it down to St. Paul street, and to build it in the shape of a Maltese Cross, but for many reasons, the plan had to be resigned in favor of the present building, the length of which is 255 feet 6 inches,

COURT HOUSE—See page 32.

C

and its breadth 144 feet 6 inches. The height of the towers is 220 feet. The great window at the high altar, which is filled with beautifully stained glass, is 64 feet high and 32 feet wide. The church is capable of accommodating over seven thousand persons. In the northeast tower is a fine chime of bells, and in the north-west tower is placed the largest bell in America, cast expressly for this church, and weighing 29,400 lbs. ; its sound is very remarkable. This tower is open to the public for a small fee ; from the top a splendid view of the River St. Lawrence, the island of Montreal, St. Helen's island, Victoria Bridge, and the surrounding country, is presented.

SEMINARY OF ST. SULPICE, in connection with the Parish Church, is one of the most ancient buildings in the city. There is a public clock in the front of the building, equally celebrated for its antiquity. Nearly opposite the Seminary are the Rooms of the Cercle Littéraire.

OTTAWA STREET.

WESLEYAN METHODIST CHURCH is a neat stone building, services in which are, for this part of the city, well attended.

NEW CITY GAS COMPANY'S WORKS. corner of this and Ann street, is well worthy a visit, the works being very extensive. The Company have recently erected a new meter-house, in which has been placed a new meter capable of measuring many million feet of gas. It was manufactured at the celebrated works of Thos. Glover, manufacturer, of London, England.

POINT ST. CHARLES.

WESLEYAN CHURCH. The style adopted is early English, and the materials used in the superstructure are red, white, and black bricks, with Ohio rubbed sandstone, water tables, string courses, and dressings to openings, with tesselated tile sands. A central doorway leads to the main hall, which communicates with the school-room and with the body of the church, by steps ascending right and left. The tower is surmounted with a spire covered with tin. The roof is framed with open timbers, stained and varnished.

ST. MATTHEW'S CHURCH is a neat brick building, used by the Presbyterians in connection with the Church of Scotland.

SHERBROOKE STREET.

BON PASTEUR NUNNERY, a large stone building, devoted to the care and shelter of the aged and infirm of the R. C. persuasion is situated near the junction of Sherbrooke and St. Constant streets. This institution, like most others of the same class in the city, has a chapel attached to it.

WESLEYAN CHURCH, at the corner of St. Charles Borrommee street, is a handsome edifice in the English Gothic style, with a tower and spire rising from the front to the height of 120 feet. The roof is covered with different colored slates. The interior has an arched roof, grained oak. There are no galleries except at the end. The pews are curved, which adds much to their beauty, and is a great convenience, since by it the congregation in every part face the preacher. Behind the pulpit there is an organ gallery, in a recess, with a neat pointed arch and columns in front, and underneath this gallery is the vestry. The church has three entrances in front, and one in the rear, and a lofty basement extends under the whole edifice, forming school, class, and lecture rooms, vestry, &c.

McGILL COLLEGE is beautifully situated at the base of the mountain, and immediately in front of the Reservoir. This establishment owes its origin to the liberality of the late Hon. James McGill, who bequeathed the estate of Burnside and £10,000 for its endowment. Besides lecture, class, and other rooms, it contains residences for its professors. A new wing has lately been erected by William Molson, Esq., to be called the "Molson Wing." Its different schools of medicine, law, arts, &c., bear a very high reputation. Principal J. W. Dawson, Esq., LL.D., F.G.S., &c.

McGILL COLLEGE.

MAGNETIC OBSERVATORY. A cut stone octagonal building, with a low tower, surmounted by a dome, for the accommodation of Dr. Smallwood's valuable collection of astronomical and other apparatus; it is attached to and situated on the grounds of the McGill College.

R. C. THEOLOGICAL COLLEGE is erected on the ground belonging to the seminary of St. Sulpice, commonly called the "Priests' Farm," abutting on the line of this street, from where a good view of the building can be obtained. It is an extensive and imposing structure, in the

Italian style. The plan forms three sides of a quadrangle, having the wings advancing. The building is capable of accommodating a very large number of boarders, and contains a chapel 100 by 40, with a library above it. Rev. C. J. Delavigne, Director.

ST. ANTOINE STREET.

Passes west from Craig street into the suburbs, and the farther it goes the more is taste displayed in the buildings, it being inhabited by many of the wealthier classes. At the west end it comes very close to a precipitous rock which rises up between it and Dorchester street. There are gardens laid out with terraced walks here and there. The sidewalks are shaded by rows of trees, which give a cool and refreshing shelter from the heat of the sun's rays.

RICHMOND SQUARE, at the upper end of this street, and close to the stopping place of the city cars, is a very neat square, occupying a large space at both sides of the street. The grounds are very nicely laid out, with a fountain in the centre of each square.

ST. BONAVENTURE STREET.

COLONIAL CHURCH AND SCHOOL SOCIETY MODEL SCHOOL. A large brick building entered through an iron gate directly opposite Little St. Antoine street. This is one of the best common schools in the Province, and is conducted on Episcopalian principles.

MERCANTILE LIBRARY. The frontage of the building is 54 feet, and from the pavement to the top of the cornice 58 feet. It is built of Ohio sandstone above the basement course, which is of limestone. The elevation presents a handsome appearance, consisting of three storeys of various designs, as to window openings and other details. The general outline of the building or plan is that of an H, and consists of two main portions, connected by a spacious hall going the entire length of the structure, and from a wide staircase on one side of the latter access is given to the various rooms on each storey. The entrance to this hall is in the centre of the facade, and thirteen feet in width. In the rear portion of the building on the ground-floor will be found three large rooms, consisting of a board-room and two class-rooms, and the whole of these can be thrown into a fair sized lecture room, or place for holding meetings of an ordinary character. Facing the staircase, in the centre of the building, is a room well adapted for a class-rom or office of good size. The height of this storey is 14 feet 6 inches clear. On the first floor, fronting St. Bonaventure street, is the reading-room, 50 feet long, 40 feet wide, and 17 feet in height, with an entrance from the front hall or landing. The library is in the rear portion of the building, and is 48 feet by 28, and of the same height as the reading-room. Between these two rooms, and separated from them and the hall by glazed partitions, is the librarian's office. From the latter entire super-vision is obtained by the librarian over the whole of this floor, no person being able to enter or leave either the reading-room or library, or go up or down stairs without his knowledge. The second or top storey is to be devoted in front to a lecture room for members of the association, of the same size and over the reading room, while in rear, over the library, will be found a well-proportioned and effectively lighted room, intended for a picture gallery or museum. The light during the day time is obtained from the large skylight in the centre of the room, while at night ample provision is made for a large number of gas-burners, arranged in the best possible manner for throwing an equal and good light upon the pictures or other objects on exhibition. The main stair-case terminates on this level, and opposite to it, and between the lecture-room and picture-gallery, is a room suitable for an office in connection with the picture-gallery, or for a small private reading-room, &c. The height of this storey is about 17 feet. The lavatories and other con-veniences will be provided for in the lofty and airy basement storey. The entire building is heated by steam.

GRAND TRUNK RAILWAY DEPOT, better known as the "Bonaven-ture Street Station," is a large building built of brick in the usual "Depot" style, containing ticket and other offices. All trains leaving the city start from this depot.

ST. CATHERINE STREET.

ASILE DE LA PROVIDENCE, an institution conducted by the nuns, devoted to the care of the aged and infirm.

ST. JAMES' CHURCH (R. C.), a large stone building on the corner of this street and St. Denis street, 120 feet long, and 35 feet deep, three storeys high, with a pitched roof, is under the control of the clergy of St. James' Church, and has accommodation for about 600 boys.

SALLE D'ASILE, a Roman Catholic school for the education of the blind, a large brick building, inside a wire fence. It is conducted by nuns.

FIRE STATION, No. 5, a brick building in the style of all our smaller fire stations, and, like them, it communicates with the Fire Alarm Tele-graph.

PHILLIPS' SQUARE, a small plot of ground of very unprepossessing appearance, used principally as a "short cut."

CHRIST'S CHURCH CATHEDRAL (C. of E.) at the corner of University street, is a beautiful edifice in the mediæval Gothic style. The plan is cruciform, and is indeed a model of ecclesiastical architecture. The tower and spire—the latter of which is well proportioned and springs

MERCANTILE LIBRARY—See page 37.

gracefully from the former—are at the intersection of the four arms of the cross, and measure 224 feet in height. The church is built of Caen stone and Montreal limestone. Length of the building inside, 187 feet, width of nave 70 feet; transept, including tower, 99 feet. The upper stage of the tower contains a peal of bells, and the clocks are placed immediately above the corbel-table. The windows are good and copied from the best mediæval English churches. The front entrance is beautifully designed—in fact the building is unequalled on this continent.

EXHIBITION BUILDING, was originally erected for the reception of the Prince of Wales, and since 1860 has been used for various purposes.

ERSKINE CHURCH (*Canada Presbyterian*). Style, English Gothic. The building is 134 feet by 82 over projections, 90 feet from ground to apex of roof, 50 feet height inside. Tower 120 feet high, with spire 185 feet. Sitting accommodation is afforded to 1,200 people. Pastor, Rev. Dr. Taylor; assistant, Rev. Mr. Gibson.

PROTESTANT ORPHAN ASYLUM, is a neat stone building, and one of the most useful as well as the best conducted institutions in the city, and is sustained by the benevolence of private individuals.

CHURCH OF ST. JAMES THE APOSTLE (C. of E.), is the Protestant church furthest west in the city. Its appearance outside is very fine, being built of Montreal stone, in a simple and chaste Gothic style of architecture. The length is 115, the width 45 feet, and the height from floor to apex of roof 60 feet. It has no ceiling, but the roof presents a variety of stained wood, its elegant arches resting on corbels of dark Montreal and white Ohio stones, which mingle together in striking contrast. At the end of the church stands a memorial window to Prince Albert; besides this there are five stained glass memorial windows. A handsome tower and spire have been added to this church, as a memorial from Mr. and Mrs. Charles Phillips to a deceased brother. The tower is distinct from the main building, and has a connecting corridor, through which is the principal entrance to the church on the west side. In the lower storey of the tower there are three stained glass windows, one as a memorial, the other two containing the armorial bearings of Mr. and Mrs. Phillips. In the third or upper storey are placed a clock and a peal of bells. The spire is constructed of wood and galvanized iron, finished with a handsome vane. The total height from the ground to the top of the vane is 130 feet

ST. CONSTANT STREET.

JEWISH SYNAGOGUE. The first regularly built synagogue in British North America which has been erected for the Jews of the Polish, German, and English ritual, and one of the handsomest buildings of the kind on this continent. It is built in the Grecian style of architecture, and both in its exterior and interior finish a perfect gem of architectural beauty.

ST. DENIS STREET.

VIGER SQUARE GARDEN is the finest and most extensive in the city, neither pains nor expense having been spared to render it an attractive spot. Four basins with fountains have been constructed; as also has a very handsome, though small, hot house. A very desirable improvement, in the way of a drinking fountain, has been added to the many other progressive features of this garden. The band of one of the regiments in garrison plays here for a couple of hours, once a week, sometimes oftener, during the summer months.

TRINITY CHURCH (C. of E.) This magnificent edifice is in the early English style of Gothic architecture, and built of Montreal stone, the body of the work being natural face coarsed ashlar. The weatherings, quoins, &c., are finely dressed; the roof is covered with slate; the spire is wood, covered with galvanized iron, and, together with the tower, rises to the height of 200 feet. The lower part of the tower forms the principal entrance porch, and there are in addition two side entrances, giving access as well to the galleries and basement. The length of the church inside is 114 feet, the width 65 feet. The chancel, which is in the form of an apex, is 36 feet by 23 inside. The nave is 40 feet wide, and has a grained ceiling rising to a height of 52 feet. The side aisles in which there are galleries, are 12 feet 6 inches wide, and have pannelled plaster ceilings, with the roof timbers exposed. The body of the church is lighted by 12 windows, each terminating in traced heads, and clerestory windows formed in the roof. The church is said to afford accommodation for over 4,000 persons. Under the church is a capacious basement, 14 feet high, well lighted, and having three distinct entrances. It contains a lecture room 100 feet long by 64 feet wide, library, vestry, and all the necessary accommodation for schools, &c.

ST. JAMES' CHURCH (R. C.) This handsome building is erected upon the ruins of the one destroyed by the great fire of 1852, known as the Bishop's Church, which was of the Roman-Ionic style, but altered in form and extended in length, is now built after the most admired specimens of the early pointed style, chiefly drawn from existing examples of the thirteenth century; it is a fine example of what is sometimes called Christian architecture. The windows are of stained glass.

DEAF AND DUMB INSTITUTION. This is a fine large stone building, above Sherbrooke street, devoted, as its name infers, to the education of the deaf and dumb. It is open to visitors, and is conducted by nuns.

ST. DOMINIQUE STREET.

GERMAN CHURCH. This is a neat, though small, edifice, opposite the St. Lawrence Market, used by our German Protestant fellow citizens.

CHURCH OF ST. JAMES THE APOSTLE—See page 41.

ST. FRANCOIS XAVIER STREET

Is remarkable only as being the "Wall Street" of Montreal, chiefly famous, of course, as being the resort of brokers, money-changers, lenders, &c., &c.

ST. GABRIEL STREET.

CANADA HOTEL. A large, convenient, second-class house, very well conducted, and much frequented.

NEW CITY GAS WORKS. The office of these works is situated in this street, at the corner of St. James.

GAREAU HOTEL. A house more used as a first-class boarding house than as a hotel, and is much frequented by the legal fraternity at luncheon hour.

ST. GABRIEL CHURCH (C. of S.), is a plain stone building, and will seat about 800. This is one of the oldest Scotch churches in the city, and is under the pastoral guidance of the Rev. Mr. Campbell.

MUSEUM OF THE GEOLOGICAL SURVEY is a large building facing the end of the Champ de Mars. The museum contains samples of stones, coals, fossils, snd all the other materials that contribute to form a geological museum, and is under the direction of the celebrated geologists, Sir William E. Logan and Dr. T. Sterry Hunt. The museum is really well worthy a visit.

ST. JAMES STREET

May be called the Bond street or Broadway of Montreal, its spacious breadth and numerous fine buildings entitles it to the first rank among our city thoroughfares. It is perhaps seen to more advantage from the corner of McGill street, whence the fore-shortened line of uniform and lofty stone buildings, terminating in the perspective of the portico of the Bank of Montreal, and the more ornate erections in its vicinity, have a very fine effect. The buildings most worthy of note are the:

CITY BANK, a handsome cut stone building, in the Grecian style of architecture.

BANK OF MONTREAL, opposite the Place d'Armes, an elegant cut stone edifice, with six massive ornamental columns; is one of the finest examples of Corinthian architecture to be found on the Continent of America.

LIVERPOOL AND LONDON INSURANCE Co.'s BUILDING, is an elaborate pile of stone, containing the offices of the Company, and the City and District Savings Bank.

LA BANQUE DU PEUPLE, is a rather good looking cut stone building, on the corner of St. Francois Xavier street.

POST OFFICE, a handsome building, and in the very heart of the (business) city. The dimensions are a front of fifty-four feet on St. James street, and one hundred feet on St. Francois Xavier street, with a height of fifty-seven feet. It is designed in the Italian style. It has three stories and an attic, all of which are heated in winter by a hot-air apparatus placed in the basement. The great hall is seventy feet long, fifty feet wide, and sixteen feet high, with a fine pannelled ceiling, supported by six hollow iron pillars, which are used for conveying the heated air to the upper stories.

ST. LAWRENCE HALL, (Hotel,) a fine cut stone building, well finished, without as well as within. This well-known house is regarded as the most popular and fashionable hotel in the Province, and has been under the charge of its present proprietor, Mr. Hogan, for upwards of ten years. The Building has over 325 apartments, a large number of which were occupied by the suite of H. R. H. the Prince of Wales on the occasion of his visit in 1860.

BANK OF BRITISH NORTH AMERICA, is a fine cut stone building, in the composite style of architecture.

COLONIAL LIFE ASSURANCE COMPANY'S BUILDING, is a striking pile of handsomely finished cut stone buildings, occupied by the Company's offices, and the ground floor by the Banque Jacques Cartier.

PRINTING HOUSE, one of the oldest buildings in the street, but which has lately had a new shop front put in, and been otherwise renovated, making it one of the handsomest stores in the street. The shop is occupied by Mr. Alex. McGibbon, grocer, and is called the "Italian Warehouse"; the other part of the building is occupied as the office of the "Montreal Gazette" and "Evening Telegraph" newspapers, and M. Longmoore & Co., Book and Job Printers.

WESLEYAN CHURCH is an elegant edifice in the florid Gothic style of architecture of the 14th century. Its size is 111 by 73 feet, and it will seat about 2,300 with comfort. The arrangement of the interior is unique and beautiful; the pulpit especially calls for notice, being a fine specimen of the carved Gothic style. This church contains one of the finest organs in the city, the supply of wind for which is worked up by water power.

MOLSON'S BANK. This building was carried out under the able and experienced supervision of George and John Jas. Browne, Esqs., Architects, whose design was unanimously adopted after a competition. The structure has three frontages or facades, faced with Ohio sandstone. The shafts of the Doric columns of the portico (ground floor,) and those of the Corinthian columns forming the centre of the second storey on the Great St. James street front, are of polished Peterhead granite, the red tint of which has a fine effect. The principal entrance to the

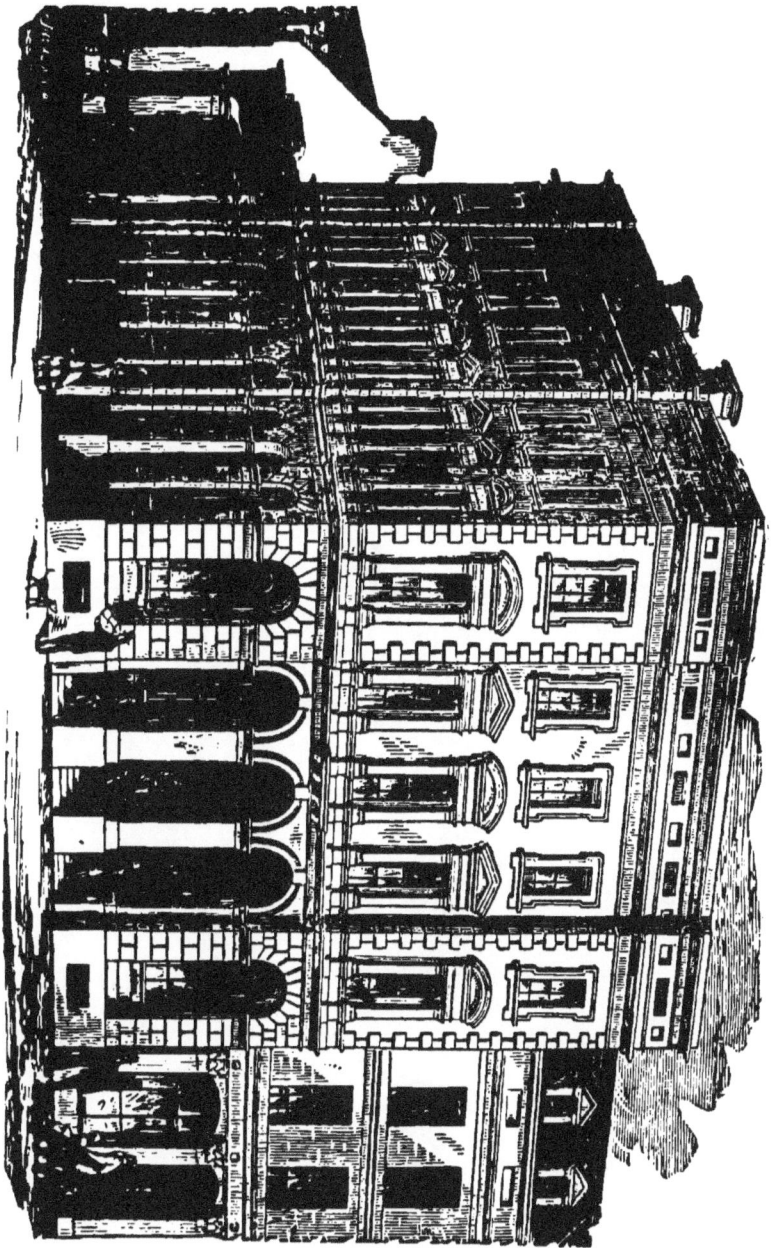

POST OFFICE—See page 46.

bank is in the centre of the ground floor of this front, and the private entrance in the east or court facade, entered from the same street. The third front, in St. Peter street, has a separate and independent entrance to commodious chambers which occupy the first and second floors, and are to be leased to public companies as offices. The street facade possess, not only from their extent, but from their architectural treatment, a bold and imposing character, and display in their composition, appropriateness and simplicity, the general forms conducing to unity and expression of purpose. They are also remarkable for the boldness of their projections, and interesting as showing the tendency at the present moment to the use of a much larger amount of carving for external decoration than has hitherto been employed. The substructure of the principal facade on Great St. James street is a stylobate of massive vermiculated rustic, from which rise broad pilasters or rusticated piers on either side of the central projection or portico which extends to the street line, the whole including one tier of openings, and surmounted by a regular Doric entablature. Of the five compartments into which the ground floor of this facade is divided, the central one is somewhat wider than the rest, and displays a handsome entrance doorway of large proportions and deeply recessed, approached by a flight of steps externally. The windows have semicircular heads, radiating rustics, moulded jambs, carved imposts and masks on the key stones. The doors are constructed of plate iron with oak framings, cast iron mouldings, with ornaments and medallions bolted thereon, and finished to imitate bronze. The sashes to the ground floor throughout are of Spanish mahogany, varnished and polished, and glazed with single sheets of plate glass. The shutters are of plate iron, in two parts, balanced and adjusted so that when the upper half ascends the lower one descends into grooves constructed in the wall to receive them, and *vice versa*, when the upper part descends, the lower one ascends, and both meet in a groove in the centre of the height of each window, where they become locked. An entablature, marking the separation of the second storey from the third or attic storey, and projecting forward in the centre of the building over the four Corinthian columns, is enriched with modillions and dentils to correspond in richness and effect with the capitals of the columns. The upper part of the building is terminated with an attic cornice, breaking forward with the centre of the building, which corresponds in width with the portico on the ground floor. Thus the effect of a centre, indicated by the projecting portico on the ground floor, is maintained throughout the whole height of the building, and, being surmounted by a sculptured group, forms the most prominent feature in the composition. Another noticeable feature in this building is the stacks of chimneys carried up above the attic cornice, which are executed in rubbed sandstone, and are of an ornamental character.

COMMERCIAL BANK, on the corner of St. Peter, is a plain cut stone building, in the Grecian Doric style.

MECHANICS' INSTITUTE. This handsome structure at the corner of St. Peter street, has a frontage of 64 feet on Great St. James, by 100 feet on St. Peter street. It is designed in the Italian style, and forms one of the architectural ornaments of Montreal. The ground floor contains two large and handsome shops, the next contains a corridor, reading room, library, president's, committee and class rooms. From the corridor on this flat three staircases lead to the third story, which forms a very handsome concert or lecture hall, which is tastefully fitted up, has a good sized platform at one end, is well lighted by gas and can seat over 1,000 persons. S. M. Sansum, Superintendent.

OTTAWA HOTEL, a fine stone building close to McGill street, and contiguous to all the public resorts, is one of the oldest hotels in Canada, enjoys a good reputation, and, we believe, deservedly. Burnett & Doyle, proprietors.

VICTORIA SQUARE, at the foot of this street, is a very fine enclosure, being well fenced in and planted with flowers and shrubs, the walks and beds being in excellent order; in the centre is a large stone basin containing several jets of water.

THE ST. JAMES HOTEL, long known as the Bonaventure Building, is situated at the south-west side of the above square, and being a peculiar combination of brick and stone, arrests the attention of most persons. It has a frontage of 50 feet on the west side, 90 feet on the south-east, and 60 feet on St. Bonaventure street, making a total frontage of 210 feet, with nine different entrances. It is 80 feet high, consisting of five storeys, having an iron railing around the roof, from which a magnificent view of the whole city and surrounding country is presented. There is a large clock in the main front of the building, the public benefit of which is duly appreciated by the community at large. It is well fitted up, and its management gives general satisfaction. Hogan & Co., proprietors.

ST. JOSEPH STREET.

ST. GEORGE'S CHURCH is a very neat building, in the style of the 13th century. It is of rough stone, with towers and a handsome flight of stone steps at the main entrance. The interior is fitted up in a chaste and elegant style, and has an excellent organ. The building is 150 feet in length by 56 feet in width, and will seat over 1,500 persons. Is under the pastoral charge of the Rev. William Bond, LL.D., and the Rev. Jas. Carmichael, A.M.

DOW'S BREWERY. A large building on the corner of this and Colborne streets. Is the most extensive brewery in the country, and its celebrated manufactures are well known throughout Canada.

PRESBYTERIAN CHURCH, at the corner of Seigneurs street, is a very neat brick building, and is adapted to seat about 500 persons.

STANDARD LIFE ASSURANCE COMPANY'S BUILDING.

See page 46.

WESLEYAN CHURCH, opposite the last mentioned, is a neat and commodious stone building. It was opened for worship this year (1870).

CANTIN'S SHIP-YARD. One of the most celebrated yards in the Province. Is worthy a visit.

THE WESTERN ROYAL SCHOOL, situated on St. Joseph, between Workman and Delisle streets, was opened by Prince Arthur, in February, 1870. It is a substantial, handsome, three-storey brick building, with abundant room for heating, ventilation, and everything to secure the comfort and health of the scholars. It is attended by from 500 to 600 children. Principal of boys' department, Mr. Laing; of girls' department, Miss Bothwell.

ST. LAWRENCE MAIN STREET.

This is the main avenue leading to the Mountain and Mount Royal Cemetery, and is the principal business street in the St. Lawrence suburb. There are a large number of fine buildings, principally dry goods houses, with, at the upper end, many private residences. The City Horse Railway cars traverse this street as high up as the toll-gate.

ST. MARY STREET.

CITY PASSENGER R. R. Co. The chief stables and station of this company are situated below the toll-gate, and are well worthy a visit. The station is adapted for an innumerable number of cars, and the stables are capable of accommodating about 130 horses. There is also a machine shop and an office with dwelling for superintendent and foreman. The company have a number of other stables on the different branches of their track. From opposite this station the Current Ste. Marie commences to be very troublesome to vessels coming up the river, at times four steam tugs being necessary to tow a vessel to the wharves.

THE JAIL is a substantial stone building, surrounded by a high stone wall. It is comparatively a new edifice, and cost over $120,000. Parties wishing to see the interior can do so by obtaining an order from the Sheriff to that effect.

MOLSON'S BREWERY AND DISTILLERY is one of the institutions of Montreal, and one of the most extensive establishments of the kind in the Province.

PAPINEAU SQUARE, formerly a large piece of uneven ground without the slightest attraction, has of late years been considerably improved in appearance.

PAPINEAU MARKET, a large brick building fitted up in the same style as most of the other markets, with divisions for fowl, fish, flesh, &c. It is situated in Papineau Square.

MOLSON'S COLLEGE is a large quadrangular brick building, originally built with the intention of becoming a first-class college for both sexes, and to bear the name of its founder, the late T. Molson, Esq.; this scheme not succeeding, the building was leased to Government as a barrack. Is is now vacant.

ST. THOMAS CHURCH (C. of E.) This church was built by the late T. Molson, Esq., at his sole expense. It is a neat brick building, having a tower with a clock in the centre. Incumbent, Rev. Mr. McLeod.

ST. NICHOLAS STREET.

LOVELL'S PRINTING OFFICE. The most extensive printing establishment in the Province. The presses are all worked by steam. The buildings are heated by steam, and furnished with every convenience which skill has devised. When we say that it is from this house the celebrated Canada Directories of 1857 and 1870, and also the first-class Canadian educational series now so generally used throughout the country are issued, we need not further praise the energy or public-spiritedness of the proprietor, Mr. John Lovell, who is at all times willing to allow parties to visit the premises.

ST. PAUL STREET

Is the principal *Wholesale* business street in the city, and contains in various portions of it numerous lofty and elegant warehouses, to which additions are constantly being made. It being impossible in our limited space to particularize, we shall direct the visitor's attention merely to the *Public* buildings.

BONSECOURS CHURCH (R. C.) The oldest in the city, having been erected in 1658; it was burnt in 1764, but rebuilt in 1771. It contains a good organ, and will seat about 2,000 persons; there is a building used as a school connected with the church.

BONSECOURS MARKET. A magnificent pile of stone, in the Grecian-Doric style of architecture; has a front of three storeys on Commissioners street; cost about $300,000, and is equal to any building of the kind in America. It consists of a large butchers' market, extending almost the whole length of the building, over which is a fine concert hall, the council room, and the various offices of the Corporation, including that of the fire-alarm telegraph, the wires of which may be seen converging to a circular frame on the roof, from all parts of the town. Beneath the butchers' market is a large basement devoted to pork, cheese, vegetables, and fish, for the latter of which a separate portion has been allotted and fitted up in the best style with marble slabs, fountains, drains, and thorough ventilation. Bonsecours Market presents a lively scene on market days, when the farmers congregate; the stranger is amused by the quaintness of their costumes, and the abundance of gestures they exhibit, as they press their wares upon the customers.

MOLSON'S BANK—See page 46.

Victoria Barracks, or Nuns' Buildings. A magnificent block of stone buildings, originally intended for stores, but lately used as barracks. The Grenadier and Scots Fusilier Guards occupied these barracks during their sojourn in Canada.

ST. SACRAMENT STREET.

Merchants' Exchange. This fine building, the "Rialto" of Montreal, is situated in this, one of the narrowest streets of the city, and is consequently seen to great disadvantage. The premises cover an area of somewhat less than half an acre, which comprises an open court used as an entrance to the Corn Exchange and other offices. The building contains a reading room, the Board room and offices of the Board of Trade, and many other public and private offices of a commercial nature.

Corn Exchange—facing this street and extending from St. John to St. Alexis streets—is a large brick and stone building, admirably adapted both in dimensions and architecture to the purpose for which it was built.

Montreal Telegraph Company's Office, a substantial looking stone building, like its opposite neighbour, the Merchant's Exchange, is subject to the disadvantage of being in a very narrow street. It however presents a very good appearance

UNIVERSITY STREET.

Museum of the Natural History Society, is a pretty large brick building in view of the English Cathedral. The managers have got together a very large and good collection, particularly of the Canadian species. This institution is well worthy a visit.

VISITATION STREET.

St. Peter's Church (R. C.), is a very handsome cut-stone building, in the style of the 13th century, and will accommodate over 3,000 persons. A handsome cut-stone building is attached to it, being the residence of the clergy in connection with this church.

WATER STREET.

Military Hospital. This a is large stone building, enclosed by a high stone wall, and almost projecting over the wharf in the rear. This is a very good situation for a hospital, if for no other reason than having plenty of fresh air from the river.

Quebec Gate Barracks, occupied by two batteries of Royal Artillery, and detachments of the Commissariat and Engineer corps. These buildings formerly, under the old French rule, belonged to a nunnery.

WILLIAM STREET.

G. T. R. CARTAGE Co's STABLE. This is a very large brick building, erected by Shedden & Co., for the accommodation of their own horses, and is about the largest building of the description in Montreal. It is ventilated by means of eight shafts running through the roof.

ST. MARK'S CHURCH (C. of S.), corner of this and Dalhousie streets, is a neat, commodious edifice, fitted up to accommodate about 350 attendauts. Rev. Mr. Black, pastor.

BONSECOURS MARKET—See page 54.

PUBLIC WORKS, &c.

THE LACHINE CANAL, which extends for 8½ miles, from the Harbour of Montreal to Lachine, has kept pace with the general progress of the city ; a large new dock has just been built outside the lock at Windmill Point ; a large new dry-dock has also recently been completed by Mr. Cantin, the capacity of which is sufficient to take in any vessel navigating the canals. Mills, foundries, and in fact all manufactories requiring water power are rapidly springing up on its banks.

NEW CITY GAS WORKS were incorporated in July, 1847. Its capital is $300,000. Building, corner of Ottawa and Dalhousie streets.

WATER WORKS. The water is taken from the St. Lawrence about one and a-half miles from the Lachine Rapids, where the elevation of the river surface is about 37 feet above the Harbour of Montreal. The Wheel-house at the termination of the aqueduct is worthy of notice. The water is admitted to and discharged from this building through submerged archways under covered frost proof passages, extending above and below the building. There are two iron wheels, twenty feet in diameter, and twenty feet broad. These wheels are upon the suspension principal, "high breast" or "pitch back," with ventilated buckets. These reservoirs are excavated out of the solid rock, and have a water surface of over ninety thousand square feet, 206 feet above the harbour, with a depth of 25 feet. The length is 623 feet, with a breadth of 173 feet, formed into two reservoirs by a division wall. The two contain about fifteen million gallons. Total cost of aqueduct, machinery, pumping-main, and reservoirs, about $1,800,000.

FIRE ALARM TELEGRAPH was recently erected, and has proved a thorough success. The chief office is in the City Hall, from which it has connections with 60 boxes, the church bells, several public clocks, the Observatory and Water Works near McGill College.

VICTORIA BRIDGE. This gigantic structure, which was inaugurated by H. R. H. the Prince of Wales, in August, 1860, spans the St. Lawrence at Point St. Charles, the terminus of the Grand Trunk Railway.

It is one of the most stupendous and massive structures of modern times. It is tubular, consisting of 23 spans of 242 feet each, with the exception of the one in the centre, under which the steamboats pass, it being 330 feet wide. The dimensions of the tubes are 19 feet high at the extreme end, rising to 22 feet in the centre tube, by 16 feet wide. The Bridge is approached at each end by a causeway terminating in abutments of solid masonry. The southern causeway is 240 feet long, and the northern 1,400; the width of each being 90 feet. The total length of the bridge is 2 miles, less 50 yards,—250,000 tons of stone and 8,000 tons of iron were used in its construction. The total cost was $7,000,000. By this bridge two extensive and populous sections of country are united, thus adding to their social, agricultural, and commercial development.

THE EMIGRANTS' BURIAL GROUND is a large square enclosure at Point St. Charles, in view of the Bridge; it is planted with trees, having a large boulder in its centre, placed on a cut stone base, and bearing an appropriate inscription to the memory of the emigrants that perished of ship fever in 1847.

GRAND TRUNK RAILWAY. The chief offices of this Corporation are situated at Point St. Charles, and are very extensive, consisting of machine shops, engine rooms, freight and car sheds, with all other accessories. A fine view may be had from the small bridge which leads to the chief offices; the Mountain, the Victoria Bridge, the River, &c., are all seen to great advantage from this position.

FRENCH MISSION CHURCH—See page 24.

DRIVES, &c.,

IN AND AROUND THE CITY.

ROUND THE MOUNTAIN. This is considered the favourite drive. The distance round is nearly nine miles. The general route is up the St. Lawrence Main Street, past the toll-gate, off to the left, and gradually up the Mountain side. Arriving at a branch road which leads to the Mount Royal Cemetery, we take the road to the right and continue our course till we arrive at Cote des Neiges, which pretty little village lies nestled in the bosom of the mountain, and sheltered by its branching arms from North and East. Leaving the village we drive on up the grade and gradually reach the summit, at which a toll-gate is placed. Here we are quite shut in on all sides, but as our vehicle turns the curve, we cannot refrain from indulging in many exclamations of admiration. There, almost at our feet, lies the city, with its spires, its houses, its streets. There also is Canada's pride, the Victoria Bridge, the Nun's Island in its glorious verdancy, the glittering river, with many gallant vessels, which after battling the breeze, now lie quietly at the wharf, either loading or discharging their cargoes. There also is St. Helen's Island, and behind it the spires of the church in Longueuil village. The base of the mountain almost all around is adorned with many elegant villas, the palatial summer residences of our merchant princes. The choicest orchards of Lower Canada are also situated around it, the fruit being of the most delicious flavor and great luxuriance of yield. Taken as a whole, this is one of the most pleasant drives in Canada.

MOUNT ROYAL CEMETERY is one of those places of interest which travellers should never neglect to visit. It is a very pleasant drive of about two miles from the city on the mountain road. The cemetery lies in a very picturesque position in the valley between the two mountains. Lofty, wide, and imposing entrance gates, first meet the view; inside these gates, on the right, is a handsome and substantial residence for the superintendent; on the left a small but pretty church. The lofty pointed pinnacles of the entrance gates, the high pitched roofs of the house and church, with the bell turret and gabled windows are in perfect

E

keeping with the surrounding scenery and the luxuriant foliage of the trees. The "Molson" vaults and monuments are the handsomest as well as the largest on this continent, and will well repay the time and small expense necessary to enjoy a drive through the extensive and well laid out grounds.

LACHINE ROAD. This is a very pleasant drive, going out by St. Joseph street to the toll-gate, passing which we are on what is called the Upper Lachine road. At each side of us are the farms of our market gardeners and others. A road leading from this takes us to Cote St. Paul, where there are a number of factories and very pretty church called—

THE UNION CHURCH. This, one of the prettiest little churches on the island, was erected some years ago on a commanding site facing the locks of the Lachine Canal, in the Gothic style of architecture, constructed of red, white, and black bricks, ornamented tesselated tile sands, &c. The main entrance is in the tower, which forms the northwest corner of the building, and is surmounted by a spire.

We leave Cote St. Paul and pass through the small villages of the Tanneries, Blue Bonnets, &c., and arrive at Lachine, a village once well known, it being the residence of the late Sir George Simpson, the Governor of the Hudson Bay Company, and also the point from whence all orders were dispatched to the many posts of the Company throughout their vast territory. Returning to town we take the Lower road, which is directly along the bank of the river, presenting scenery of unsurpassed beauty and grandeur; we see the Lachine Rapids boiling, foaming and dashing in their wild fury from rock to rock, from crevice to crevice. If the proper hour is selected for this truly delightful drive, a view may be had of the descent of the steamer through those rapids.

LONGUE POINTE ROAD. This is another favourite drive along the river side, down St. Mary street, through the toll-gate to the village of Hochelaga, the quarters of a portion of the garrison, and in which are two pretty little rural churches, one Protestant, the other Roman Catholic; continuing down this road we arrive at a large commanding-looking building, the Convent of the Holy Name of Mary. Passing on a few miles further we arrive at *Longue Pointe*.

BACK RIVER ROAD is another drive. It leads to Monklands (the Maria Villa Convent), which was formerly the residence of the Governor General. There is a very handsome church in connection with this convent. This road also leads to Isle Jesus, and many other pretty villages.

LACHINE RAPIDS are situated opposite the Nun's Island, and nearly half-way between the city and the village of Lachine. The tourist should take the cars for Lachine, starting from the Bonaventure street.

station at 7 o'clock A.M., and take the steamboat at Lachine to descend the rapids. Running a rapid is at all times an exciting circumstance, whether it be done in a birch bark canoe on a small river, or in a steamer on the mighty St. Lawrence. When the steamer approaches the rapid, a pilot, skillful, experienced, and specially chosen for the purpose, takes charge of the wheel, extra hands stand by to assist, while others go aft to the tiller, to be ready to steer the vessel by its means should the wheel tackle by any accident give way; the captain takes his place by the wheelhouse, ready with his bell to communicate with the engineer; the vessel plunges into the broken and mad waters, she heaves and falls, rolls from side to side, and labors as if she were in a heavy sea, the engine is eased, and the steamer is carried forward with frightful rapidity. Sometimes she appears to be rushing headlong on to some frightful rock that shows its bleak head above the white foam of the breakers; in the next instant she has shot by it and is making a contrary course, and so she treads her way through the crooked channel these mad waters are rushing down. A few moments suffice for this, and the smooth green waters are reached again, then all breathe freely, for none but old and experienced pilots can run the great Rapids of Lachine but with bated breath. A slight Rapid called Norma Rapid is then passed through, and after shooting under that great monument of engineering skill, the Victoria Bridge, and past the Canal Basin, the steamer lands her passengers at one of the wharves at about 9 o'clock, just in time and with a good appetite for breakfast.

St. Helen's Island, which, were it not for the white tents seen among the trees, no one would ever suspect to be a strong military post, but which probably holds more shot and shell in its cool underground magazines than would blow all the Island of Montreal to atoms, is one of the prettiest spots near Montreal, and is open to the public, who can gain admittance by a pass from the Town-Major.

GRAND TRUNK RAILWAY.

Two express trains leave Montreal daily—morning and evening—for Toronto, Hamilton, Detroit, and all points west.

About the beginning of June it is expected that Pullman's splendid Palace Cars, also new and improved first-class Coaches, will run on all Through Express Trains between Portland and Detroit.

For particulars as to times of arrival and departure of all trains to and from the city, the reader is referred to the *International Railway Guide*, which contains correct and reliable time-tables of all the routes.

The office of the Grand Trunk Railway is at 39 St. James street, Montreal.

CANADIAN NAVIGATION COMPANY.

One of the steamers of this line leaves the Canal Basin, Montreal, at 9 A.M., daily (Sundays excepted), and Lachine on arrival of the train leaving the Bonaventure station at noon, for Hamilton and the intermediate ports. The arrangements of its first-class steamers are of the completest kind, ensuring every comfort and the greatest dispatch.

The Company also supply tourists during the season with an opportunity of visiting Murray Bay, Riviere du Loup, Tadousac, and the Saguenay, on whose natural beauties it is unnecessary to dwell. In the early part of the season, the " Union," and in the latter, the " Magnet," make the trip from Quebec to the Saguenay, touching, of course, at the intermediate points.

The office of the Canadian Navigation Company is at 73 St. James street, Montreal.

THE RICHELIEU COMPANY.

This Company own the daily Royal Mail Line of Steamers running between Montreal and Quebec. The splendid iron steamers "Quebec" and "Montreal" leave the Richelieu pier, opposite Jacques Cartier Square, Montreal, alternately every evening during the season for Quebec, calling at intermediate ports. In everything likely to conduce to comfort and to enhance the pleasure of travelling, this line is, we do not hesitate to say, certainly unsurpassed by any on these waters.

The office of the Richelieu Company is at 201 Commissioners street.

MUIR'S BUILDING, Notre Dame Street.

CITY COUNCIL.

HIS WORSHIP THE MAYOR,
WILLIAM WORKMAN, Esquire.

WARDS REPRESENTED.

East Ward .... BETOURNAY, PLINGUET, WILSON.
Centre Ward .... CHRISTIE, BERNARD, LYMAN.
West Ward .... NELSON, ALEXANDER, R. H. STEPHENS.
St. Ann's Ward .... McGAUVRAN, RODDEN, McSHANE.
St. Antoine Ward .... MASTERMAN, KAY, THOMPSON.
St. Lawrence Ward .... TAYLOR, DEVLIN, G. W. STEPHENS.
St. Louis Ward .... DAVID, LEDUC, HENDERSON.
St. James' Ward .... RIVARD, ST. CHARLES, BASTIEN.
St. Mary's Ward .... DESMARTEAU, JORDAN, SIMARD.

OFFICERS OF THE CORPORATION.

JOHN P. SEXTON, City Recorder.
CHS. GLACKMEYER, City Clerk.
JAMES F. D. BLACK, City Treasurer.
P. MACQUISTEN, City Surveyor.

F. W. PENTON, Chief of Police.
H. I. IBBOTSON, Clerk Recorder's C't.
WM. ROBB, Auditor.
A. BERTRAM, Chief Engineer Fire D

TARIFF FOR HACKNEY CARRIAGES.

PLACES.		Two or Four Wheeled Carriages drawn by one horse.		Coaches or Four Wheeled Carriages drawn by two horses.		TIME ALLOWED.
FROM	TO	For one or two persons.	For three or four persons.	For one or two persons.	For three or four persons.	
		$ cts.	$ cts.	$ cts.	$ cts.	
Any Place.	Any other in the same division & back.	0 15	0 25	0 30	0 40	½ an hour.
		0 5	0 00	0 00	0 00	
Any Divi'n.	Any place in another division and back	0 25	0 40	0 40	0 50	¾ of an hour. over ¾ of an hour & under 1 hour.
		0 35	0 50	0 60	0 75	
Any Place.	(Per Hour.) Any other in the City.	0 50	0 70	0 75	1 00	One hour. For every additional ½ hour
		0 20	0 30	0 30	0 40	

Reasonable weight of Luggage allowed free of charge.
Children under 12 years of age to be charged half-price.

DIVISIONS OF THE CITY.

The First Division comprises the East, Centre and West Wards, (including the South-West side of McGill Street, and the North-West side of Craig Street.)

The Second Division comprises the St. Ann, St. Antoine and St. Lawrence Wards (exclusive of McGill and Craig Streets.)

The Third Division comprises the St. Louis Ward, (exclusive of Craig Street), the St. James and St. Mary's Wards.

VALUES OF SILVER COINS.

United States Half Dollar	- -	47 cents or	2s. 4d.
Do	Quarters - - -	23 cents or	1s. 2d.
Do	Ten Cents - - -	9 cents or	5d.
Do	Five Cents - - -	4 cents or	2½d.
Do	Three Cents - -	2 cents or	1d.
British Shillings - - - - -		24 cents or	1s. 2d.
Do Sixpence - - . - - -		12 cents or	7d.
Canadian Silver at Par.			

FIRE DEPARTMENT.

Chief Engineer—A. BERTRAM, cor. Craig and Chenneville streets.
Assistant Engineer—WM. PATTON, 312 Lagauchetiere street.

FIRE ALARM TELEGRAPH.

Chief Operator—F. H. BADGER.

DISTRICT NO. I.

1. Custom-House, (North Corner.)
2. Cor. St. Jean Baptiste and St. Paul sts.
3. Jacques Cartier sq., (cor. St. Paul st.)
4. Court House sq., (Hose Station.)
5. Cor. Notre Dame and St. Francois Xavier sts.
6. Cor. St. Sacrament and St. Peter sts.
7. Cor. St. Paul and McGill streets.
12. Cor Craig and Chenneville sts. (Central Hose Station.)
13. Cor. Craig street and St. Lambert Hill.
14. Cor. Vitre and Sanguinet streets.
15. Cor. St. Lawrence and Lagauchetière streets.
16. Cor. Dorchester and St. Urbain streets.
17. Cor. Bleury and Dorchester streets.
18. Beaver Hall Hill.
19. St. Antoine street, (opp. Geneviève st.)
21. Cor. Brunswick and Dorchester streets.
23. St. Catherine street, (Hose Station.)
24. Cor. St. Lawrence and St. Catherine sts.
25. German street, (Hose Station.)
26. Cor. St. Catherine and St. Denis sts.
27. Cor. German and Ontario streets.
28. Cor. St. Lawrence and Sherbrooke sts.
29. Cor. St. George and Sherbrooke streets.
31. Cor. Union avenue and Sherbrooke st.
32. Cor. McGill College avenue and St. Catherine street.
34. Guilbault's Garden.

DISTRICT NO. 2.

35. Cor. King and Common streets.
37. Cor. Duke and Ottawa streets.
38. Cor. Dupré lane and St. Maurice sts.
39. Cor. St. Antoine and Cemetery streets.
41. Chaboillez square. (Hose Station.)
42. Wellington street, (Hose Station.)
43. Mill street, (Lyman's Mills.)
45. Cor. Wellington and McCord streets.
46. Cor. Colborne and Ottawa streets.
47. Cor. St. Joseph and Mountain streets.
48. Cor. St. Antoine and Mountain streets.
49. Cor. St. Catherine and Mountain streets.
51. Cor. Sherbrooke and Peel streets.
52. Cor. St. Antoine and Guy streets.
53. Cor. St. Martin and St. Bonaventure sts.
54. Cor. St. Joseph and Canning streets.
57. Cor. William and Seigneur streets.
61. Redpath's Sugar Refinery.
62. St. Gabriel Market, (Hose Station.)
63. Grand Trunk Works, (Pt. St. Charles.)

DISTRICT NO. 3.

64. Cor. Notre Dame and Bonsecours sts.
65. Dalhousie square, (Hose Station.)
67. Cor. Wolfe and St. Mary streets.
72. Cor. Craig and Visitation streets, (Hose Station.)
74. Cor. Dorchester and St. André streets.
75. Cor. Mignonne and St. André streets.
76. Cor. Amherst and Ontario streets.
81. Cor. Robin and Visitation streets.
82. Cor. St. Catherine and Panet streets.
83. Papineau Market.
91. Jail Gate, (St. Mary street.)
92. Cor. St. Mary and Dufresne streets.
93. Cor. Ontario and Fullum streets.

TIME AND DISTANCE INDICATOR.

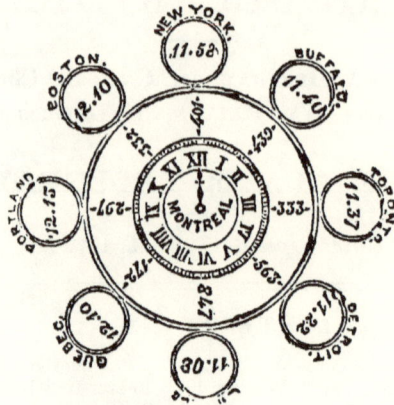

TRAINS ARE RUN

Between Portland and Island Pond, by Portland Time.
    "   Island Pond and Montreal, by Montreal Time.
    "   Rivière du Loup   "   "   "
    "   Rouse's Point   "   "   "
    "   Province Line   "   "   "
    "   Montreal and Toronto   "   "
    "   Toronto and Sarnia,   by Toronto "
    "   Fort Erie and Goderich   "   "
    "   Port Huron and Detroit   by Chicago "

TABLE OF DISTANCES.

Montreal to Liverpool, England	2750	miles.
" to Kingston, P. O.	173	"
" to Quebec, P. Q.	180	"
" to Toronto, P. O.	333	"
" to Halifax, N. S.	815	"
" to Rouse's Point, U. S.	44	"
" to Portland, "	292	"
" to Boston, "	333	"
" to New York, "	403	"
" to Cincinnati, "	964	"
" to Chicago, "	1040	"
" to St. Louis, "	1345	"
" to Omaha, "	1533	"
" to Ogden, "	2565	"
" to Sacramento, "	3309	"
" to San Francisco, "	3447	"

ST. LAWRENCE HALL,

ST. JAMES STREET,
MONTREAL.

H. HOGAN, - - - **Proprietor.**

This First-Class Hotel, the largest in Montreal, is situated on St. James Street, in the immediate vicinity of the French Cathedral, or Church "Ville Marie," Notre Dame Street, adjacent to the Post Office, Place d'Armes, and Banks; is only one minute's walk from Grey or Black Nunneries, New Court House, Reading Rooms, "Champ de Mars" (where the troops are reviewed), Mechanics' Institute, Bonsecours Market, and the Fashionable Stores.

The new Theatre Royal is directly in rear of the House, and several of the best boxes are regularly kept for guests of this Hotel.

The St. Lawrence Hall has long been regarded as the most

POPULAR AND FASHIONABLE HOTEL IN MONTREAL,

and is patronized by Government on public occasions, including that of the visit of

H. R. H. THE PRINCE OF WALES AND SUITE,

AND THAT OF

HIS EXCELLENCY THE GOVERNOR GENERAL AND SUITE.

During the past winter the Hotel has been considerably enlarged, so that in future the Proprietor hopes to be able to accommodate comfortably all who may favour him with their patronage.

All Rooms lighted by Gas.

The Consulate Office of the United States is in the Hotel, as well as a Telegraph Office to all parts.

The Proprietor begs to announce that having recently purchased the St. Lawrence Hall property, it is his intention next Fall to pull down and re-build, with all the modern improvements, including an Elevator; thus making this Hotel second to none in the United States.

ST. JAMES HOTEL,

MONTREAL.

The Undersigned beg to notify the Public that they have purchased the above well-known FIRST-CLASS HOTEL, and which is now carried on as a

BRANCH ESTABLISHMENT

OF THE

ST. LAWRENCE HALL.

UNDER THE MANAGEMENT OF

Mr. SAMUEL MONTGOMERY, and Mr. FRED'K GERIKEN,

(*Nephew of Mr. Hogan.*)

Both well known to the travelling community in the United States and Canada, as being connected with the St. Lawrence Hall.

The ST. JAMES is very favourably situated, facing Victoria Square, in the very centre of the city, and contiguous to the Post Office and the Banks.

Its convenience for BUSINESS MEN is everything that can be desired, as it is in the immediate vicinity of the WHOLESALE HOUSES.

The Rooms being well appointed and ventilated, are cheerful for FAMILIES, while the *menage* will always be unexceptionable, and no pains spared in ministering to the COMFORT OF GUESTS.

The Proprietors having leased the adjoining Premises, are prepared to offer every inducement to the SPRING AND FALL TRADE; and as their tariff is unexceptionably reasonable, they hope to obtain a large share of public patronage.

H. HOGAN & CO.

LOCKMAN'S PATENT.

The Lockman is the greatest improvement of the Age.

IT IS A PERFECT SEWER

Never out of Order.

More durable and cheaper than any other First-Class Machine.

LOCK STITCH FAMILY SHUTTLE SEWING MACHINE.

EVERY MACHINE WARRANTED ONE YEAR.

OVER 3,500 SOLD IN CANADA IN LAST FIVE MONTHS.

GEO. HARVEY,
343 NOTRE DAME ST.,

DEALER IN

ALL KINDS SEWING MACHINES.

SOLE AGENT, Province of Quebec.

REPAIRING PROMPTLY DONE AT LOW PRICES.

AGENTS WANTED
TO WHOM LIBERAL INDUCEMENTS ARE OFFERED.

J. H. DICKINSON,

IMPORTER AND MANUFACTURER OF

GENTS' SHIRTS,

COLLARS,

TIES, AND HOSIERY,

19 PLACE D'ARMES SQUARE,

MONTREAL.

White Dress, Regatta and Oxford Shirts,

MADE TO ORDER IN 24 HOURS.

A PERFECT FIT GUARANTEED.

F

THE

INTERNATIONAL

RAILWAY AND STEAM NAVIGATION

GUIDE,

TIME TABLES OF ALL CANADIAN RAILWAYS

THE PRINCIPAL RAILROADS IN UNITED STATES,

Maps of the Principal Lines

AND

Condensed Time Tables of Through Express Trains Between all Important Points;

ALSO,

INLAND STEAM NAVIGATION ROUTES,

TOGETHER WITH

RAILWAY TRAFFIC RETURNS AND MISCELLANEOUS READING
INTERESTING TO THE TRAVELLER.

CAREFULLY COMPILED FROM OFFICIAL SOURCES, AND PUBLISHED SEMI-MONTHLY.

For Sale by all News Dealers and Booksellers; also by News Boys on
Trains and Steamers, and at the principal Railway Depots throughout
Canada and the adjoining States.

PRICE 10 CENTS.

PUBLISHED BY C. R. CHISHOLM & Co.

GENERAL NEWS AGENTS,

MONTREAL.